D1580538

Cultivating
Prayer&
Intercession
In The Local Church

Nine Principles That Release
The Church to
"Pray Without Ceasing"

Dr. Mark S. Jones

Published by City Bible Publishing
9200 NE Fremont
Portland, Oregon 97220

Printed in U.S.A.

City Bible Publishing is a ministry of City Bible Church and is dedicated to serving the local church and its leaders through the production and distribution of quality restoration materials.

It is our prayer that these materials, proven in the context of the local church, will equip leaders in exalting the Lord and extending His kingdom.

For a free catalog of additional resources from City Bible Publishing please call 1-800-777-6057 or visit our web site at www.citybiblepublishing.com.

Cultivating Prayer & Intercession in the Local Church
Nine Principals That Release The Church to "Pray Without Ceasing"

ISBN 1-886849-93-5

All scripture quotations, unless otherwise indicated, are taken from

New King James Version. Copyright © 1982 by Thomas Nelson, Inc. Used by Permission. All rights reserved.

New International Version. Copyright © 1973, 1978, 1984 by the International Bible Society. Used by permission of Zondervan Publishing House. All rights reserved.

Called to Pray

In this new millennium, God's desire is to raise up Interceding Churches. Throughout time there have been those who have heard the call to prayer, and there have been previous prayer movements. Yet again today God is calling His Church to prayer.

Cultivating a pure heart toward prayer is a process. The parable of the sower (in Matthew 13 and Mark 4) illustrates that the important issue with God is the soil quality of the heart. As in any earthly garden, the garden of our heart must be cultivated, planted and maintained before beautiful results come forth. **For a local church to be fruitful in prayer, people's hearts must be right. Hindrances to the praying church are directly related to issues of the heart.**

When the seed, which is the Word of God, cannot take root due to the hard soil condition, it can't even begin to grow! A church with hard ground will not respond to the Word of God regarding prayer. Rocky soil represents an insecure life. The withering plant symbolizes a believer unable to cope under difficult circumstances. God wants to deal with all these situations and, by His grace, see His people through to victory. Thorny ground is a heart of "mixture" (worldly cares and natural distractions). Focusing on the Lord Jesus, rather than the temptations of life, enables the single heart to come forth in prayer.

After the soil of our hearts has been prepared, the seed of the Word of God regarding prayer must be planted through teaching, preaching, inspiration, impartation, and practice. The plant grows as faith is stirred and encouraged by the Word. Some water, some fertilize, but God causes the growth. Then begins the maintenance aspect of the garden of prayer. Individually and corporately, God is calling us to tend our gardens with the utmost care, bringing forth productivity in prayer, increase upon increase.

In the local church we can observe three levels of prayer: no prayer, some prayer, or lots of prayer. Amazingly, there are churches with 'no prayer' activity. Though they hold prayer as a doctrinal truth, it is not practically applied.

Other churches function with 'some prayer'. Within a limited level of revelation, they give prayer a measure of importance. There may be a group of intercessors, yet many in the church lack an awareness of the need to pray, or of the need for prayer.

The church with 'lots of prayer' is well on its way to becoming an interceding church. The people are thinking prayer in every situation. Their leaders cry out to the Lord for wisdom on how to, *"pray without ceasing." (I Thess. 5:17)* **As the church touches God in corporate prayer, He is able to come through with miracles.** Dynamic faith that inspires individuals to trust God is now developing entire congregations into prayer warriors. Interceding churches are raised up one person at a time, with every member contributing faith to fuel a great movement of prayer.

Be ready to receive new keys to unlock prayer in the local church. Before you read another word, go get a notebook and pen. Title it "Cultivating Prayer and Intercession in the Local Church". Every time you get something from the Lord, write it down. When you have finished reading this book, go back over your notes. You will be surprised how much God has given you. Take what you have and do it! You will be well on your way to raising up an interceding church. Be patient, be diligent, be humble, and watch God do the rest. Start now, read on, and write down the vision. *(Hab.2:2-3)*

PRAYER PRINCIPLES

It is God's heart to see His church a 'House of Prayer for all nations'. Only churches with a foundation of prayer can reach their full potential in God. The following nine principles will help you lead your congregation on the priceless journey of prayer and intercession. As each is understood and released into the hearts of God's children, prayer will begin to blossom. No longer a drudgery, prayer and intercession will be the most exciting part of their Christian experience.

❧ A P P R E C I A T I O N ❧

Our prayer is that this little book will be a true blessing to you. I especially want to thank my wife Susan, for without her efforts this book would not have been possible. Because of her dedication my thoughts have finally become reality on paper.

My deepest appreciation to Pastor Frank Damazio for releasing Susan and me into the wonderful work of Prayer Ministries. There is no greater joy in our lives than serving the local church with our family.

Thanks to Kathy or making sure all the t's were crossed and i's were dotted.

A big thank you to Jim and Laura, who applied not only their layout and writing expertise, but for putting their hearts into this book.

It would not have been possible without the dedicated prayers of our intercessors. Thank you Jim and Terri, Bill and Vicki, Lowell and Barb, Matt and Irena, Jay and Rosie, and all the others who stood by our side and held our hands up. We all know "Nothing can happen except by prayer." Our heart's desire is to serve our Lord Jesus by serving the local church, and thereby seeing the Kingdom of God extended on the earth.

May this little writing encourage and enrich your life.

Dr. Mark S. Jones

Restoration of the Altar of Incense

In this prophetic season, God is restoring the Altar of Incense to the life of every believer and every Local Church. *"And.....(they) fell down before the Lamb.* **Each one had a harp and they were holding golden bowls full of incense, which are the prayers of the saints."** *(Rev. 5:8)* God is causing His people to arise. Prayer and intercession should be a pivotal part of life in Christ, from devotional prayer to warfare prayer.

The Old Testament Tabernacle of Moses is a divine pattern, revealing the necessity of God's presence. *"Then have them make a sanctuary for me, and I will dwell among them."* *(Ex. 25:8)*

We are admonished to build the House (dwelling place for God's presence) according to the pattern found in Exodus 35 - 40. Proceeding from the outside of the tabernacle, the furniture appears in a specified order. In the Outer Court are the Brazen Laver and the Brazen Altar. The Golden Candlestick, the Table of Shewbread, and the Golden Altar of Incense are in the Holy Place. The Ark of the Covenant rests in the Most Holy Place.

"Incense always speaks to us of the prayers and intercession of the saints, which ascend unto God. They begin on the Altar, with man, and as they burn, they ascend upward to God. Likewise our prayers begin in the heart of man and ascend heavenward unto God."[1]

Psalm 141:1-2 implores, *"O LORD...Hear my voice when I call to you.* **May my prayer be set before you like incense; may the lifting up of my hands be like the evening sacrifice."**

The Altar of Incense parallels our personal prayer lives. In Exodus 30:1-10, God said to make it out of acacia wood, (Christ's humanity) overlaid with gold (Christ's divinity) and four horns (power). It was the highest piece of furniture in the Tabernacle, representing our highest calling in Christ. The Altar was to be constantly tended, with the lamps trimmed and incense burned every morning and every evening. It was to be positioned before the veil, immediately before the Holy of Holies and the presence of the Lord.

The only true incense that God desires now is that which ascends from the heart. He is interested in prayers, worship, praise and intercession that come from the spirit. *"God is spirit, and his worshippers must worship in spirit and in truth." (John 4:24)*

We in the New Covenant are Kings and Priests, who are to offer incense through prayer. *"You have made them to be a kingdom and priests to serve our God, and they will reign on the earth." (Rev. 5:8-10)* A priest is a person who intercedes on behalf of another. *(I Pet. 2:9)* "The Bible teaches that we are to pray in the spirit and by the spirit. True incense is that which arises from the believer's heart, ascending within the Heavenly Sanctuary, Jesus Christ. When we send up incense to the Lord, our whole nature and being must be involved. **We must be saturated and permeated with the fragrance of prayer life, and the fire of the Spirit will cause our incense to ascend.** God places a high premium on prayer." [2]

The Church is called to be "a House of Prayer" for all nations, *(Mark 11:17)* and to pray and make intercession for all men. *(I Tim. 2:1)* The obvious plot of the enemy is to try to steal our prayers by removing the altar of incense, the prayer life of the believer. If the enemy accomplishes this task, the key weapon for successful Christian living is lost. *"For though we live in the world, we do not wage war as the world does. **The weapons we fight with are not the weapons of the world. On the contrary, they have divine power to demolish strongholds.** We demolish arguments and every pretension that sets itself up against the knowledge of God, and we take captive every thought to make it obedient to Christ." (II Cor 10:3-5)*

The enemy can steal the believer's prayer life through a variety of means. Ignorance, sin, or a guilty conscience will turn a warm heart cold. Indifference, apathy or a cold heart toward God can stifle prayer. Feelings of inferiority or condemnation can have a devastating effect on a person's ability to pray. Sound Biblical teaching helps to solve these issues. Distraction and the business of life can squeeze out prayer, yet a fresh prioritizing of time can remedy this source of prayerlessness.

God desires to restore prayer passion in every believer. All over the world churches are burning the true incense day and night, giving birth to the plans and purposes of God in the earth today. How is your personal altar of incense? How is the altar of incense in your church? What is the Holy Spirit saying about what is rising from your life?

Intercession:
Not an Office or Gift,
But the Function of Every Believer

P astor Frank Damazio, in his profound teaching "Gap Standing, Hedge Building", dispels the myth of exclusiveness regarding prayer and intercession.[3] He reinforces the truth that intercession is the function of every believer. The New Testament list five offices for governing the local churches. Intercession is not listed among these offices. *"It was he who gave some to be **apostles**, some to be **prophets**, some to be **evangelists**, and some to be **pastors** and **teachers**, to prepare God's people for works of service, so that the body of Christ may be built up."* (Eph. 4:11-12)

The Apostle Paul, a dynamic intercessor, understood the necessity of prayer to move the Kingdom of God forward here on earth. We are to imitate Paul in his zeal to equip, impart and instruct the Body in prayer and intercession. *"Whatever you have learned or received or heard from me, or seen in me... put it into practice."* (Phil. 4:9)

Neither is intercession listed with the gifts. *"There are different kinds of **gifts**, but the same Spirit. There are different kinds of service, but the same Lord. There are different kinds of working, but the same God works all of them in all men. Now to each one the manifestation of the Spirit is given for the common good. To one there is given through the Spirit the **message of wisdom**, to another the **message of knowledge** by means of the same Spirit, to another **faith** by the same Spirit, to another gifts of **healing** by that one Spirit, to another **miraculous powers**, to another **prophecy**, to another **distinguishing between spirits**, to another speaking in* *different kinds of* **tongues***, and to still another the* **interpretation** *of tongues. All these are the work of one and the same Spirit, and he gives them to each one, just as he determines." (I Cor. 12:4-11)*

Some have taught it as a gift, but when we look, it's just not listed in reference to the gifts of the Spirit. I believe it is not there for this reason: a gift is given to some and not necessarily to others. It is not that way with prayer. Prayer is available to all.

It is then safe to assume that intercession is a function of every believer, just like that of worship. Worship is not listed in the gifts or offices; yet every Christian knows that God tells us all to worship. In the area of prayer and intercession, like that of worship, some may give themselves to greater study and skill development, but all believers are called to be thus involved. All are to worship. All are to pray. It is not for a select group, but the function of every believer to rise to the place God has for him or her in prayer.

This understanding opens up a whole area of truth that has been lost to the local church. Reducing prayer down to the responsibility of a 'gifted' few effectively moves the church toward a state of prayerlessness. Those who feel 'gifted' to pray are often the prophetic types who receive frequent 'insights' from the Lord. In their attempt to give these insights to the pastor, often they are not received. This can bring feelings of misunderstanding and rejection, leading to backbiting and gossip.

The principle that everyone is an intercessor releases all believers to the work of prayer, restoring a healthy balance in the local church. It is foundational to the raising up of an interceding church. Jesus is our example. Paul is our example. The whole church must follow suit. Let us never again return to the limited perspective that intercession is an office or a gift. It is the function of all believers! This truth, taught to the local church, will do more to release the Church into effective prayer and intercession than any other truth.

If you are a Senior Pastor reading this book, do your congregation a great service by releasing them into prayer. Like Lazarus, they are bound. You have the ability to set them free in prayer. When you do, ask God for the grace for prayer and intercession to fall on your church.

Prayer, the Most Resisted Activity on the Planet

It is imperative to understand the warfare involved in prayer. Developing prayer is a lot like rolling large boulders uphill. Have you noticed? The devil doesn't want prayer to be an active part in the local church. He doesn't want to see those boulders moved! We must be dedicated to moving prayer forward no matter how difficult it is. Fight off discouragement. Realize that every inch of forward movement takes the local church to new levels of prayer and intercession and greater victories for the Kingdom of God. *"The thief comes only to steal and kill and destroy; I have come that they may have life, and have it to the full." (John 10:10)*

The enemy works to steal, kill and destroy prayer. If he can steal it, he will then try to kill it. If that works, he will try to destroy it. He will make every effort to render an individual or congregation prayerless, which equates to powerlessness.

Notice how in Daniel's life *(Dan. 6)* his daily prayer came under attack. He prayed three times a day, connecting him to the source of his power. He was favored of God, and the men that opposed him tried to cut him off from that power source. They proclaimed a decree making it, in effect, illegal to pray. Of course Daniel obeyed the higher law when he continued to pray, yet he was still thrown to the lions. The enemies' plot was foiled when God intervened and shut the mouths of the lions. I believe the attack came upon his prayer life because prayer was his connection to God.

In observing prayer and intercession in the local church, and in the lives of individuals, I have become convinced that prayer is resisted at 3 levels:

To Pray   The Prayer   The Answer

As you observe prayer in your local church, whether in the individual or in a specific department, these three levels will always come into play. If the enemy can stop an individual at any level, he will certainly try. **Our job is to persevere and press in until the answer comes.** This is often difficult due to the element of the unseen and the time delay factor that occurs between the prayer and the answer. Thus, many people need assistance in reaching the point of breakthrough: 'The Answer'.

TO PRAY...

The first level where prayer is resisted is the level 'To Pray'. It is an essential part of spiritual discipline. Have you ever set a date to meet with the Lord, only to have that time stolen from you? Have you ever planned to upgrade your devotional times and found that EVERYTHING worked against your doing it? The alarm failed to ring, you had to work overtime, and an emergency arose. You are getting the picture. There is resistance to the activity of prayer.

Resistance also comes through false stereotypes. Whom do you imagine as an intercessor? An older woman? That would signify an age or gender distinctive. A retired missionary? That is a ministry distinctive. Someone a little peculiar or odd? Now we are using a personality distinctive. And last, did you think of someone whose prayers are long, aggressive and loud? That is a style distinctive. In essence, anyone else but 'who I am' is what the enemy would have you to think. Prayer and intercession are not for a certain personality type, gender, ministry or style, but rather for all believers.

Take a moment now, and think about all the ways prayer is resisted in your own life and the life of your church. In the face of resistance, we can stand on the promise that 'greater is He that is in you, than he that is in the world'. Jesus, the greatest Intercessor, will help us in our endeavor to see the church reach her full potential in prayer.

THE PRAYER...

The second level of resistance is 'The Prayer', the actual opening of your mouth. Many are fearful of speaking out in prayer, whether in the prayer closet or in a prayer meeting, either because of the fear of failure, or not knowing exactly what or how to pray. The resistance at this point is very real. It may consist of a lack of wisdom (how to pray), or just a lack of specific details. So often, people don't know what to 'say'.   Maybe they are OK with silent prayer, but praying out loud in a group setting would be out of their comfort zone. Jesus was very specific, and taught his disciples to pray with these words: *"When you pray, say..."*. *(Luke 11:2)*

The enemy has been successful in keeping the Christian silent, but Jesus wants our prayers to be verbalized. Resistance comes when self-consciousness enters. For the local church to be released in prayer and intercession, every believer must become comfortable 'saying' their prayers. Fear of failure, or the fear of man, is often the root cause. Participating in frequent times of spoken prayer will help diminish self-consciousness. Even non-believers, when in a dangerous or difficult situation, will call out in prayer to God for "help". The Lord hears these prayers.

One man in a Church Membership class shared how he had been changed by verbalized prayer. (At City Bible Church we begin every service with 15-20 minutes of prayer, which includes a time for small group prayer throughout the sanctuary.   This allows everyone to pray out loud in a small group, even though there may be a couple of thousand people present.) On his first Sunday, he joined a small prayer group of 4 or 5 people standing around him. Never having prayed with anyone out loud in his life, he was terrified. But he stepped out in faith and prayed for the needs of another person in his group that morning. He actually opened his mouth in prayer! The next Sunday he got up for church and hurried his wife along, telling her, "We've got to get to church on time! I don't want to miss the prayer part." What had happened? This man had touched God in a new way. Prayer was not just an event for him; it was an encounter. He became an intercessor as he stood in the gap for another's need.

THE ANSWER...

The third level of resistance is in the 'The Answer'. When there is a delay with no apparent answer, there is a tendency to give up. Daniel 10:12-13 relates, *"...Do not be afraid, Daniel. Since the first day that you set your mind to gain understanding and to humble yourself before your God, your words were heard, and I have come in response to them.* **But the prince of the Persian kingdom resisted me twenty-one days.** *Then Michael, one of the chief princes, came to help me, because* **I was detained there with the king of Persia."**

Here we learn that even the angel of Lord fought demonic resistance. Daniel's fervent prayers were HEARD on the first day, yet the answer was delayed. What happened in the meantime? Resistance in the heavenly realms. Did Daniel know that? No. He just stood in faith, continuing in prayer for 21 days until the answer finally broke through.

Jesus gives us a New Testament example of persistent prayer in Luke 11:5-8. The neighbor needing bread to feed his guest runs next door, pounds on the door and asks for bread. Three times he knocks and asks. Persistence finally causes his friend to get up out of bed and give him the bread. Jesus likens this to prayer. He wants us to persevere in prayer, stand in the gap and build up the hedges until the answer comes. This is called the prayer of importunity - persistent prayer.

We need not be a "fast food generation" when it relates to prayer. Rather we need to persist, and when the answer does not come, persist some more! It is easy to see why this area is a point of resistance. We must strive to be overcomers.

Standing with one another in prayer is an act of encouragement, given as needed to maintain the stance of faith. *"Two are better than one, because they have a good return for their work: If one falls down, his friend can help him up. But pity the man who falls and has no one to help him up!" (Eccl. 4:9-10)* We must join arm in arm, linking our faith together as we fight. Moses depended on Aaron and Hur to strengthen him in praying for Joshua, as he fought the battle in the valley. So we need each other to stand in agreement in prayer.

Persistence and endurance are two important qualities that all members of the Body of Christ need when entering into new levels of prayer. Some battles are won quickly, while others may continue over the course of many years. The temptation to quit will stare us straight in the face, but we must stare right back because 'greater is He that is in us, than he that is in the world'.

Our pastor gave us an assignment to pray concerning some adult businesses that surround our church. When I had an opportunity to ask a national prayer leader what his plan of strategy would be in this situation, his response was simply, "Seek the Lord and do whatever he says to do." (Until then, I had been trying to come up with a plan in my natural mind to combat the giant of pornography in our city.) .

We gathered a team together and committed to pray for a strategy. The Lord gave us a plan to prayer-walk the area once a month, praying for blessing and righteousness to rule and reign. At first our emotions were high, and we had great fun doing spiritual street cleaning. We expected quick results - you know, like McDonald's. Order at the first window; pick it up at the next. That was not how things worked.

We prayed month after month, but to our surprise, another adult business sprang up. Discouraged, yes - defeated, no. Despite this setback, fruit began to appear. The two vacant buildings on nearby blocks have since been filled with reputable businesses. The police department conducted three very successful prostitution sting operations - on nights following Saturday mornings we prayer-walked! A small storefront church on the block has since relocated just down the street to a much larger facility.

After having prayer-walked for two years, the Lord challenged us to continue for three years. Three years! This project has been resisted in all three areas - to pray, the prayer, and the answer - but still it continues. Like Abraham, David and Paul, we press on.

Why is prayer the most resisted activity on the planet?

Looking through the Scriptures, it becomes quite clear. Here are twelve ways in which prayer is our connection to experiencing the blessings of God. Please search the Scriptures and find more.

1. Communion with God

"This, then, is how you should pray: 'Our Father in heaven, hallowed be your name, your kingdom come, your will be done on earth as it is in heaven. Give us today our daily bread. Forgive us our debts, as we also have forgiven our debtors. And lead us not into temptation, but deliver us from the evil one.'" (Matt. 6:9-13)

2. Peace with God - Our Salvation

"For it is with your heart that you believe and are justified, and it is with your mouth that you confess and are saved." (Rom. 10:10)

3. The Peace of God

"Do not be anxious about anything, but in everything, by prayer and petition, with thanksgiving, present your requests to God. And the peace of God, which transcends all understanding, will guard your hearts and your minds in Christ Jesus." (Phil. 4:6-7)

4. All Wisdom

"If any of you lacks wisdom, he should ask God, who gives generously to all without finding fault, and it will be given to him." (James 1:5)

5. The Keys of the Kingdom

"I will give you the keys of the kingdom of heaven; whatever you bind on earth will be bound in heaven, and whatever you loose on earth will be loosed in heaven." (Matt. 16:19)

6. Signs, Wonders and Miracles

"At the time of sacrifice, the prophet Elijah stepped forward and prayed: 'O LORD, God of Abraham, Isaac and Israel, let it be known today that you are God in Israel and that I am your servant and have done all these things at your command. Answer me, O LORD, answer me, so these people will know that you, O LORD, are God, and that you are turning their hearts back again.' Then the fire of the LORD fell and burned up the sacrifice, the wood, the stones and the soil, and also licked up the water in the trench." (I Kings 18:36-38)

7. Conflict Resolution and Physical Healing

"Is any one of you in trouble? He should pray. Is anyone happy? Let him sing songs of praise. Is any one of you sick? He should call the elders of the church to pray over him and anoint him with oil in the name of the Lord. And the prayer offered in faith will make the sick person well; the Lord will raise him up. If he has sinned, he will be forgiven." (James 5:13-15)

8. The Sword of the Spirit

"Take the helmet of salvation and the sword of the Spirit, which is the word of God." (Eph. 6:17)

9. The Holy Spirit, our Helper, Comforter, Counselor

"But the Counselor, the Holy Spirit, whom the Father will send in my name, will teach you all things and will remind you of everything I have said to you." (John 14:26)

10. Provision

"Which of you, if his son asks for bread, will give him a stone? Or if he asks for a fish, will give him a snake? If you, then, though you are evil, know how to give good gifts to your children, how much more will your Father in heaven give good gifts to those who ask him!" (Matt. 7:9-11)

11. Protection

"It was about this time that King Herod arrested some who belonged to the church, intending to persecute them. He had James, the brother of John, put to death with the sword. When he saw that this pleased the Jews, he proceeded to seize Peter also. This happened during the Feast of Unleavened Bread. After arresting him, he put him in prison, handing him over to be guarded by four squads of four soldiers each. Herod intended to bring him out for public trial after the Passover. So Peter was kept in prison, but the church was earnestly praying to God for him." (Acts 12:1-5)

12. Personal Cleansing

"Forgive us our debts, as we also have forgiven our debtors." (Matt. 6:12)

After seeing the vital role prayer is to play in both the individual's life and the life of the church, it is no wonder this area is so resisted. The often-underestimated weapon of prayer in the hand of the believer will propel the believer and the church to new levels of victory. It is time for the church to rise, move forward, and take back the area of prayer and intercession.

More Prayer is Better Than Less Prayer: Removing Condemnation

One of the tactics of the enemy in the life of the believer and church is the weapon of condemnation. **The Bible tells us that the devil is the accuser of the brethren.** If the devil can create resistance to prayer by removing it from a believer or church, great weakness will be the result. This tactic of condemnation produces guilt in the believer's life. When asked, "How's your prayer life?" or "How much do you pray?" The answer is always, "Could be better," or, "Not enough". The real question is, "How much is enough?" That is a question no one is able to answer. The devil capitalizes on the fact that much pressure has been placed on the church to pray.

"Then I heard a loud voice in heaven say: 'Now have come the salvation and the power and the kingdom of our God, and the authority of His Christ. For the accuser of our brothers, who accuses them before our God day and night, has been hurled down.'" (Rev. 12:10)

Due to this pressure, a perceived burden has been placed on the believer that he feels unable to fulfill. It can turn to a form of guilt. If not true guilt, which comes by the Holy Spirit, then the devil can use false guilt to condemn the believer. All of these negative effects impede the development of prayer in the local church. (False guilt is a very powerful negative motivator, resulting in less prayer.)

Today the Holy Spirit is releasing people from this false weight of condemnation. 'More prayer is better than less prayer' releases fresh hope in people. Where they have been bound in hopelessness and failure to pray enough, they are finding new freedom. True guilt can be brought to the cross and confessed, leading the way to a fresh start. False guilt tries to keep us in a state of condemnation, disrupting any hope of an increased prayer life. 'More prayer is better than less prayer' creates renewed vision and an ability to freely ask of the Lord, "Teach me to pray."

The disciples saw Jesus' effectiveness in His ministry to the lost. He had compassion, spoke truth, and went around doing good to all He encountered. The disciples also noticed the link between His prayer life and the outflow of good that came from His 'quiet time' with His father. They hungered to know how it worked, and asked Jesus to teach them the secret of His heart and ministry.

He responded with the teaching of the Lord's Prayer. It is simple, yet very profound. The means to get people into 'more prayer' must be love. God was motivated by love to send His Son. John 3:16 declares, "For God so loved the world that he gave his one and only Son, that whoever believes in him shall not perish but have eternal life."

Love must be the motivation behind our encouraging others to pray. No longer can guilt be used to motivate. Our love for God must drive us into Him, until the love we receive from Him flows out to the lost and dying world.

Jesus spoke of three objects of our love - love for God, love for the brethren and love for the lost. This love must emanate from Him to us, and then to others. Agape love is resident not in the emotions, but in the will, and is prompted by a deliberate choice. Love is the very nature of God. With love motivating an individual or church, nothing will be able to stop the Kingdom of God from moving forward. Love is the adhesive that keeps the church together.

The devil tries to stop love with strife and division. He fails to realize love will overcome. Jesus loves us with an everlasting love, which is the foundation of our prayer life. A love for God, His Bride (the Church), and the people who have yet to know Him is the basis for prayer. So today we repent of all false motivations to pray and receive from God the true motive - His love!

The Prayer Journey: Growing in Prayer

The disciples grew in prayer as they watched the Lord Jesus in His ministry. They were on a prayer journey, and asked Jesus, *"Teach us to pray." (Luke 11:1)* Seeing the dynamic results of Jesus' prayer life, they wanted to learn more. He taught them saying, *"Greater works shall you do because I go to the Father." (John 14:12)* The Lord wants us to be good students of prayer.

The prayer journey can be broken into four stages, showing where you are with prayer in a given area at a given time. This awareness also allows you to find out where others are. For a Prayer Pastor, organizing prayer events is exciting, but seeing people increased in their prayer life is even more fulfilling. Realizing that our intercessors needed leadership and covering, I desperately sought an understanding of prayer that could be easily imparted and communicated. Facing my own inadequacy, I cried out earnestly to God for His help. This was when the Lord led me to enter a prayer journey. Finally freed from comparing myself to others, I entered an experience that would become a lifelong pursuit. Without pressure to perform, my desire grew into a passion.

It is liberating to view prayer as a journey. There really are no limits in prayer, or in our relationship with God our Father. Thus we continue on without ever 'arriving'. We can never think we've exhausted our limits, for God is limitless. Here then is a description of the four stages of the prayer journey, as I have experienced it firsthand.

Stage 1: *No Faith*

There is a story in the Bible in which a man brings his demon-possessed son to the disciples. Yet, functioning at the point of 'no faith', they are unable to help him. Jesus takes the time to rebuke them about their lack of faith. We all have been in similar situations where our faith has diminished, leaving us feeling helpless. Can you think of a similar time in your life or ministry? Perhaps right now? The father of that boy was in a predicament. When the disciples were unable to help his son, he went straight to Jesus, crying, *"I do believe; help me overcome my unbelief!" (Mark. 9:24)*

Be brutally honest with yourself and allow the Holy Spirit to search your heart. Is there an area or two that you just can't believe God to change? You are not alone in this. When teaching on prayer, I often ask these same questions, and inevitably everyone has areas of 'no faith' to deal with. How do you know you have no faith? If there is no hope in a certain area, when a need arises you rely on your own strength, or upon fate. *"Hope deferred makes the heart sick, but a longing fulfilled is a tree of life." (Prov. 13:12)* Words spoken may also be indications of 'no faith' - our words revealing what is really in our heart. *"For out of the overflow of the heart the mouth speaks." (Matt. 12:34)*

If out of your mouth flows a constant stream of negativism, fear and complaints, you can be reasonably sure you are in the 'no faith' zone. **This is a dangerous place for a believer, because faith is the foundation of our relationship with Jesus.** When faith is eroded, our prayer life is decreased in a corresponding way.

Honesty is the best starting point. We cannot go forward until we know where we currently stand. Denial is an escape from reality. Once we encounter truth in an area, we can go forward. The man in the Bible who had a demon-possessed son pleaded for help with his unbelief. This man was honest in wanting Jesus to change an area in his life.

The Bible says it is impossible to please God without faith. As you identify areas of 'no faith' and confess them, you will discover a starting position that enables a tremendous turnaround to take place. As we stand together with faith-filled hearts, God can come and answer our plea. Identify your weaker areas, come to God in childlike simplicity, and see Him move on your behalf.

Stage 2: *Faith that God Answers Prayer*

The truth of the Word of God, related to prayer and intercession, generates faith. The believer must grow in the Word, particularly where it speaks of God's desire and ability to answer his prayer. *"Consequently, faith comes from hearing the message, and the message is heard through the word of Christ." (Rom. 10:17)*

A good heart (one with good soil) will begin to grow in the reality that God does answer prayer, today as well as yesterday. This revelation increases the faith needed to believe that God answers prayer. I encourage you, as you read through the Bible, to note each time prayer is prompted by God, and how the answer came. It is an awesome study and would certainly build your faith.

You know you are in Stage 2 when you look to someone else for prayer. It is not that you think God will not answer. You know that it is Biblical. It is just that you think He probably would not answer YOUR PRAYER. Your first reaction is to get somebody else to pray, like the pastor or some other 'prayer warrior', since you consider their prayers as much more likely to get results.

Stage 3: *Faith that God answers MY prayer*

This person is willing to pray for himself AND for others. A faith arises within, and we realize God wants to answer MY prayer. When the believer really gains 'the faith that God answers MY prayer', he becomes a threat to the kingdom of darkness. No longer does he look to others. He believes God will use him. Do not be surprised if a new level of resistance occurs. Take heart and believe the scripture: *"You, dear children, are from God and have overcome them, because **the one who is in you is greater than the one who is in the world."** (I John 4:4)*

We must be awakened, through revelation from God's Word, to the truth that God wants to use us to 'stand in the gap' for His purpose. We must believe that our prayer furthers the advancement of the Kingdom of God in our own life, and in the lives of those for whom we pray. *"I tell you the truth, whatever you bind on earth will be bound in heaven, and whatever you loose on earth will be loosed in heaven." (Matt. 18:18)*

At one memorable Saturday Night Prayer meeting, I was challenged by another couple to move out of Stage 2 into Stage 3 in my own personal prayer journey. You see, they actually believed that God answered their prayers - a new concept to me. This couple believed that when they prayed, being lead by the Holy Spirit, God would answer their prayer. They really believed it! **They did not try to create momentum, but rather listened to the voice of the Holy Spirit and prayed in accordance with His desires.** This was new to me (even though I was leading the Prayer Ministries Department), and I considered their attitude almost arrogant. Because the husband was so confident his prayers would be answered, I was about to correct him, when the still small voice of the Holy Spirit said, "Mark, I'm trying to get you there."

During the service that night, I went to the sound booth to pray for the soundman. To my amazement, the very things that had just been prayed (in the soundproof room where the prayer meeting takes place) were occurring that very moment in the service. This couple had grown to the place in their journey that they knew God answered their prayers. As a result, I've been challenged to help move as many people as possible from Stage 2 to Stage 3. This is the crossing over point. The devil tries to keep people in Stages 1 and 2, because he knows if they activate faith in God's Word, step out and believe, releasing the prayer of faith, he is in big trouble! James 5:17-18 tells us, *"Elijah was a man just like us. He prayed earnestly that it would not rain, and it did not rain on the land for three and a half years. Again he prayed, and the heavens gave rain, and the earth produced its crops."*

This is where much of the Church is today. We believe in prayer, but don't always activate the faith to pray. **Believers are often intimidated, not realizing that they might be used to accomplish great exploits for God in prayer.** The Bible says that Elijah was a man like us. He prayed and it did not rain. He prayed and it did rain. Wow! Could you pray those kinds of prayers and get those kinds of results, as you are lead of the Lord? Think about it! **Claiming such things might be considered**

extreme, yet we have to move to a larger place in prayer. In stage 3 of the Prayer Journey, the believer must step out and activate faith to believe God will answer his prayer. He must overcome intimidation. Often faith has been likened to a muscle in the body. When not used, it will atrophy. Muscles that experience resistance, such as in weight lifting or exercise, will grow and be strengthened. In applying this to prayer, one must be willing to step out of the comfort zone.

The key to raising up an interceding church is the movement of each believer from Stage 2 into Stage 3, to a place of activated faith. Remember, Jesus said even greater works will you do! Faith that God answers MY PRAYER can be the most dynamic stage the church can enter into. Since prayer is where the action is, let us move to the other side of the lake, where Jesus took his disciples into a whole new dimension of ministry.

Stage 4: *Faith to Travail*

Travailing is to receive a prayer burden from the Lord, and then carry it through in prayer until it comes to pass. This is not a style of prayer (e.g. manifestation) but a life that can carry the burden of God and be faithful to intercede until the burden is brought into being. The time this requires may be short or long.

The Apostle Paul used the illustration of childbirth to describe his prayer for the church. *"My dear children, for whom I am again in the pains of childbirth until Christ is formed in you."* *(Gal. 4:19)* As a model for this type of intercession, the process is:

- Conception: God impregnates the believer with His prayer burden, in the privacy of one's heart.
- Pregnancy: The burden grows. It may become obvious to others, who then pick up the burden as well.
- Labor: Pressure builds, and commitment to the burden increases.
- Transition: The point of no return. The answer is on the way. Pushing is necessary to see the birth take place.
- Birth: The point of fulfillment. The answer has arrived.
- The Joy: Great rejoicing over God's faithfulness in answering prayer, which releases praise, worship and thanksgiving.

Many intercessors function at this stage in the Prayer Journey. An intercessor growing into this level may feel a particular burden for a person or situation, yet not be sure what to do about it when talking with others. Be careful, because misunderstandings can result when information is shared that was not meant to be public. Jesus is clear when he says, *"But when you pray, go into your room, close the door and pray to your Father, who is unseen. Then your Father, who sees what is done in secret, will reward you." (Matt. 6:6)*

We must be able to receive His burden and take it to Him in prayer. When the burden does not lift, usually more prayer is required. This stage in prayer can bring forth the purposes of God for an individual, a church, or even a city or region. Abraham tarried in the presence of God after the others had gone, and the Lord shared with him His plans to destroy Sodom and Gomorrah. Read in Genesis 18:16-30 how Abraham had a burden for the cities and acted as an intercessor before the Lord.

People can discount their burdens, when in fact they are from the Lord. Are there areas or situations you are concerned about? How does a burden develop? How do you know it is from the Lord? God has given us the ability to discern whether something is from Him, our own thinking, or the devil. However, if the burden you receive lines up with the known will of God, such as a person's salvation, the restoration of a prodigal, a needed healing, etc., then take it to the Lord and begin to pray over the stirrings you feel.

You can never go wrong praying the will of God. Use scripture and claim the promises of God for that situation. The burden will then grow like a child grows within the mother's womb. You may feel growth, stretching, and kicking as the burden increases. Moving into Stage 4, you will become increasingly more sensitive to the voice of the Holy Spirit. At the appropriate time, the burden will be released like an infant in childbirth. Don't be surprised. As in natural birthing, the most intense time is just before the fulfillment of your intercession comes.

You may even experience physical manifestations in your body. Some intercessors do and some don't. It really isn't the focus. These manifestations have sometimes caused others to take offense or be distracted from their own prayer while praying in a group. This is when discretion is called for. It may be best to move to a more private place of prayer, especially in the corporate gathering. Even the natural birthing room is not for everyone. Remember to do all things decently and in order. When physical manifestations accompany travailing prayer, it is prudent to retreat to the private prayer closet or a small prayer group. Look not for the manifestations, but to the Lord for His will in the situation.

Never compare yourself with others, but let us all grow together in prayer and intercession. It is the earnestness of heart that is really important. Let God be God, and you just be faithful to pray until the answer comes.

Some burdens are carried over years, while others may take only a matter of days or hours. It is our responsibility to be sensitive to the Holy Spirit and leave the results up to God. Mary the mother of Jesus is another picture of this type of prayer. God placed within her the promise of the Son of God. She was impregnated with the fulfillment of the Messiah. She held on to the words the angel spoke and hid them in her heart until the appropriate time. They were concealed until she was to give birth, and the promise was fulfilled.

The local church is to be used to bring forth God's purposes here on earth. Let the Church rise in intercession to a greater level of travail and see what God will birth in reaping the harvest.

The Prayer Journey is a dynamic process. It is possible to move back and forth between stages. For example, you might have all the faith in the world for praying for finances, somewhere between stage 3 or 4. But when it comes to praying for your wayward child, you have given up and are somewhere between Stage 1 or 2. Then again, some prayers answered in that area might find you moving quickly to Stage 3 or 4 again. It could be that you have prayed for healing and the person died. Discouraged, you moved back to Stage 1 or 2 regarding healing. Maybe someone can pray in thousands of dollars, but they would not know how to pray for a prodigal child. Perhaps a church has great success in praying for political leaders, but not much in the area of deliverance. **This is where the Body of Christ comes in.** As we stand together, you can add your strong faith to my weak faith, and I can add my strong faith to your weak faith. Together we can pray to see God's will accomplished.

In the last two Stages, 'Faith that God Answers My Prayer' and Faith to Travail,' there may be a counterattack of pride. It does not take many answered prayers before the temptation to think one is somehow more spiritual than others creeps in. The only way to combat this temptation is to remember one word: HUMILITY.

"When pride comes, then... disgrace, but with humility... wisdom." *(Prov. 11:2)*

"But he gives us more grace. That is why Scripture says: 'God opposes the proud but gives grace to the humble.'" *(James 4:6)*

"For by the grace given me I say to every one of you: ***Do not think of yourself more highly than you ought, but rather think of yourself with sober judgment,*** *in accordance with the measure of faith God has given you."* *(Rom. 12:3)*

The 4-Step Prayer Journey is a reality that all believers and churches need to experience. Its foundation is faith and humility. Exercising faith, based on the truths of God's Word, and being clothed in humility will keep the believer growing in the grace of prayer. The journey will become the believer's absolute joy. It is comparable to no other natural experience. Prayer is described as the secret place. Let us all enter the 'Prayer Journey' and experience deeper fellowship with Jesus.

Pray First: Developing a Lifestyle of Prayer

As westerners, most of us wait until our backs are against the wall before praying. People who find themselves in trouble suddenly remember that God really does exist and hope that maybe He can help even them. We have all heard of the foxhole testimonies: "Lord if you get me out of this, I'll..." and then this promise is forgotten in no time at all.

Instead, prayer should be thought of as a lifestyle, offering prayer first instead of as the last resort in every situation. The simple concept of 'pray first' doesn't sound like rocket science, but it does take time and consistency to impart it into the believer's life. Once understood, a lifestyle of prayer begins. *"I urge, then, first of all, that requests, prayers, intercession and thanksgiving be made for everyone—for kings and all those in authority, that we may live peaceful and quiet lives in all godliness and holiness." (1 Tim. 2:1-2)*

The Greek word 'first' means, literally, the first thing done in order. It comes from a root in the Greek, 'protos', which means forward. Prayer is to be forward in everything. Paul's encouragement to Timothy is to cover everyone in prayer first. This might seem like an overwhelming task, but when the principle of 'pray first' is woven into the fiber of an individual or church, it really isn't that difficult at all. It could easily become the norm. Because the enemy's goal is to negate prayer, it often is left out of the equation. Paul, who understood the importance of prayer better than anyone in his day, practiced exactly what he was encouraging Timothy to do.

Jehoshaphat knew it was best to pray first when he was about to be overtaken by the enemies of Israel in II Chronicles 20:1-30. Read the passage and see how he applied prayer first, and saw the hand of God intervene on his behalf.

Jehoshaphat quickly summoned all Israel to join him in prayer and fasting as he called upon the name of the Lord. God granted them favor and gave them a strategy to use against the enemies. Just think what might have happened if they had not prayed first and received the winning plan from the Lord? What if he had gathered the leaders of that day together for a meeting to get their thoughts and opinions on how to handle this very serious situation? The result would have been dramatically different. Instead he made an announcement to inform the people of the urgent need to pray, so that they could get God Almighty's mind on the matter. Jehoshaphat made a good decision to pray first.

"Pray continually." (I Thes. 5:16) *"Do not be anxious about anything, but in everything, by prayer and petition, with thanksgiving, present your requests to God."* (Phil. 4:6) Paul is exhorting us to pray continually, and in all things pray - which equates to praying first. There is so much resistance to prayer that even this simple truth can be ignored.

When counseling and listening to people share their problems and concerns, I often ask, "Have you prayed about this yet?" In a shocking number of cases the response is "No". At first I might be amazed - until the Lord reminds me just how often I attempt to work things out on my own, without first consulting Him about it.

There are two very important basic ingredients needed in our everyday decisions: wisdom and peace. The Bible is specific in what we need to do. *"If any of you lacks wisdom, he should ask God, who gives generously to all without finding fault, and it will be given to him."* (James 1:5) How about peace? *"Do not be anxious about anything, but in everything, by prayer and petition, with thanksgiving, present your requests to God. And the peace of God, which transcends all understanding, will guard your hearts and your minds in Christ Jesus."* (Phil. 4:6-7)

If peace and wisdom are prerequisites to good decision-making, and both follow prayer, then every believer must practice the 'pray first' principle. Only then will good decision-making be a part of everyday life. Does this sound too simple? In reality, it is not as easy as it sounds. The intense warfare against prayer can make implementing this principle very difficult. You might ask, "But really, how do I apply this to my life?" In an attempt to make this as user friendly as possible, I want to share with you, out of Genesis 1:28, a concept I call the Dominion Mandate.

Dominion Mandate

God the Father has given us the mandate to enlarge and increase. *"God blessed them and said to them, '**Be fruitful and increase in number; fill the earth and subdue it.** Rule over the fish of the sea and the birds of the air and over every living crea-ture that moves on the ground.'"* *(Gen. 1:28)*

The New Testament instructs us to multiply and take care of what we are given. *"You did not choose me, but I chose you and appointed you to go and bear fruit— fruit that will last."* *(John 15:16)* *"Live life, then, with a due sense of responsibility, not as men who do not know the meaning and the purpose of life, but as those who do, make the best use of your time, despite all the evils of the days. Don't be vague, but grasp firmly what you know to be the will of the Lord."* *(Eph. 5:15-17)*

The life of any individual can be broken down into five basic areas. **We all have the same five areas to care for**. No matter what our stature or status in life, we are responsible to tend and steward each one. God wants to bless us in them. Just as a natu-ral parent wants the best for his children, our Heavenly Father wants to see us grow and mature in these areas:

1. Family

This involves all aspects of our family relationships including our relationships with our parents, extended family, our children and spouse.

2. Vocation

This would be our job, career, business, professional involve-ments and educational pursuits.

3. Ministry
This includes our church activities and commitments, evangelism, and outreach. Community service and volunteerism may be included here.

4. Health
All aspects of health are included: Spirit, Soul, and Body.

5. Finances
Everything involving money (budgets, debt, retirement, lifestyle).

In the course of pastoral ministry, I have had the opportunity to talk with a lot of people concerning their problems. No matter how complicated or serious the situations are, inevitably they all relate back to these five Dominion Mandate areas. I believe God wants to bless everyone in each of these areas. The principle of 'pray first', applied daily in each area, is crucial to receiving God's blessing. Some Christians see prayer as something to do at church on Sunday, or before meals, and not as something that can bring abundance directly into their everyday life.

We must apply the 'pray first' principle at every level of life and invite God to take Lordship. To do it on our own is to drift from that place of total dependence. The simplest truths can be unlocked with a simple prayer. Let us all pray first in our lives and see all the ways God wants to bless our five Dominion areas.

Here is another practical way in which 'pray first' can be implemented by anyone, children and adults alike. I always ask this question, "Do you want to double your prayer life?" Most people say, "Yes!" I then give people another test of two simple questions: "Do you ever experience fear? Do you ever find yourself grumbling or complaining?"

If you answered "yes" to even one of these questions, consider what Paul says. *"Do not be anxious about anything, but in everything, by prayer and petition, with thanksgiving, present your requests to God." (Phil. 4:6) "Do everything without complaining or arguing." (Phil. 2:1-4)*

We all fear and complain at one time or another. Often the carnal man will react to a situation first with fear or complaining. At the moment this occurs, let it be a red light to stop and pray. Let us ALL learn to pray first and begin to overcome fear and the tendency to complain. **Take a negative attribute in your character and turn it into a positive opportunity. There will be an immediate impact on your life.** The Bible is clear in James 3:11, concerning the importance of our words. *"Does a spring send forth fresh water and bitter from the same opening?"*

Fear, anxiety, grumbling and complaining will be defeated. God will use our prayer to bring forth life in our Dominion Mandate areas: family, vocation, ministry, health and finances. It does get easier with practice. Try it. It works! Pray first will produce amazing results.

Creating and Sustaining Momentum: Releasing Power and Anointing

All things that are accomplished by both the individual and the local church have five key steps. If momentum is stalled at any step, the fulfillment of the purpose of God may be hindered. The five steps are:

- Vision - Discern God's will in the matter.
- Strategy - Formulate a plan.
- Implementation - Carry out the plan.
- Results - Evaluate the results. Make needed changes.
- Maintenance - Ongoing care of what has developed.

There can be internal or external resistance at any or all of these levels, resulting in a real slowdown of momentum. Prayer is like the oil lubricating an automobile; it keeps all the parts moving freely. It is important to pray and cover each of these five areas consistently throughout the process.

Acts Chapter 4 is a clear example of prayer that sustained momentum (begun earlier in Chapter 2). When the disciples were being resisted in the area of preaching the gospel, they went back to prayer. Their prayers released the power of God. Prayer sustains the momentum of the church to fulfill her calling and destiny, by releasing God's anointing and hand on behalf of His purpose.

So often we start with prayer by waiting on God to receive vision and direction, only to turn that fervent seeking into programs and administration. **We are good at programs, but sustaining fervent prayer at every level is a weakness.** God wants us to stay red-hot at every level and not let the fire of prayer die out. Prayer must accompany every phase of the process, from vision to maintenance, and back again to vision. The lack of prayer at any level produces self-reliance, thus allowing the enemy to move in and hinder the work of God. Prayer at all five levels produces a dependence on God that allows Him to continue the life flow of His Spirit.

The process should look something like this:

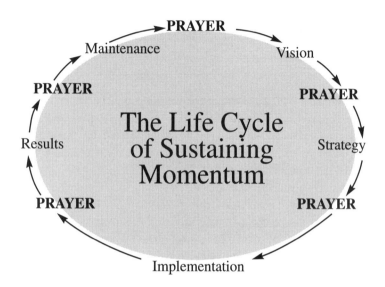

Too often, the organizational and administrative aspects of a project leave little time or energy for prayer. Regardless of whether the task originated in the Dominion Mandate, or as a ministry in the local church, the process and pitfalls are the same. The enemy understands this, and attempts to resist our prayer at each step. Scripture reminds us... *"For our struggle is not against flesh and blood, but against the rulers, against the authorities, against the powers of this dark world and against the spiritual forces of evil in the heavenly realms." (Eph. 6:12)*

The real battle takes place in the unseen world. Feelings of being overwhelmed often plague the leader who is already burdened with responsibilities. Prayer creates momentum and sustains projects to their completion. It is the secret weapon providing the necessary power to accomplish the task and reach the goal. Without prayer power, things may come to a screeching halt.

Have you ever noticed this can occur anywhere, between the receiving of a vision, all the way through the maintenance stage?

While treating a Russian missionary at the dental office, I casually asked him what kind of prayer coverage he had. He looked me square in the eye, and with a sense of seriousness responded, "I have worked eleven years to build a prayer shield and it is the lifeblood to our ministry in Russia." He said it with such conviction I was humbled and said no more. In the pause, he began to tell me the whole story. At one point in their ministry, the home church that originally sent him stopped all prayer meetings for a season. The effect was immediately felt. He was to speak at a conference but could not, because he became deathly ill. He connected it to the fact that the church had suspended its prayer meetings. The reality of answered prayer caused him to have very strong convictions regarding the value and importance of his prayer coverage.

Prayer is easily neglected. We sometimes assume that because God has called us to a particular job, He will automatically supply. That may be true, but not without a measure of resistance. **Prayer opens the door for God to move in unprecedented ways. An intercessor must be standing in the gap.**

The enemy would desire that we remain prayerless, because he understands that nothing happens except by prayer. How much prayer is necessary? More prayer is better than less prayer. The safest thing to do is to pray all 5 areas (vision, strategy, implementation, results and maintenance) until the breakthrough comes. Paul says, *"For our struggle is not against flesh and blood, but against the rulers, against the authorities, against the powers of this dark world and against the spiritual forces of evil in the heavenly realms." (Eph. 6:1)*

This battle rages; the pressure is on. Prayer is the power that releases protection, wisdom, and peace. All the resources we would ever need are available to us as we pray. We cannot underestimate the need to engage in more prayer.

∞ P R I N C I P L E   # 8 ∞

Prayer Before, During and After: Providing a Prayer Covering

T his principle is illustrated in the lives of Nehemiah and Esther. Prayer was offered before, during and after the critical events in their life stories. God intervened, and history was changed. We have seen the need to offer 'prayer before, during and after' all the events at the church.

This is true for a family situation or a mega church event. It works the same no matter where it is applied. Prayer is offered before, during and after special events and routine activities. It also includes the prayer coverage for leaders in those events.

Before: to obtain the vision and strategy, or the mind of God, in a matter. It allows for preparation in the natural and spiritual realms.

During: to move forward, to impart the vision, and to resist ungodly opposition. It moves back the darkness and opens the heavens above the situation, allowing God's blessings to flow down.

After: to give the glory to God in prayer and thanksgiving, preventing pride and self-sufficiency, as well as to prevent any counterattack from the enemy.

When visiting ministry is in our jurisdiction, it is our responsibility to prepare the way in prayer, covering them 'before, during and after'. I first learned the value of prayer 'before' in a situation when I failed to respond to the still small voice of the Holy Spirit.

One Saturday night, City Bible Church hosted a Christian artist for a concert. Being late, I was dashing across the church parking lot, when I heard the Holy Spirit ask, "Why didn't you get prayer coverage for this music group?" Not in the best of moods, I snapped back, "I can't get prayer for EVERYTHING! I am tired,

I am busy and I just cannot do it all!" The Lord very graciously said nothing more. I continued on my way to church under this overwhelming dark cloud. The next morning, when the music group got up to minister in the Sunday service, I noticed the lead singer was not singing. She had laryngitis, and the group was just beginning a tour of the U.S. In all the years of her ministry she had never lost her voice. Immediately I was convicted, and repented for not responding to the Lord's earlier prompting.

The 'during' aspect of any project or event is also very crucial. So many details need to come together in the implementation phase. Conflicts can easily interfere with an event's intended purpose, so prayer throughout is always important. Whenever the Kingdom of God is moving forward and breakthrough is imminent, resistance can become intense. The principle of prayer 'during' has been applied with great success to our Sunday morning services, with rotating Prayer Ministry teams interceding each service during the preaching.

Do not underestimate the power of prayer 'during'. Everyone benefits and everyone wins when prayer is offered up on his or her behalf. Be creative! Ask yourself these questions: "How can we cover this upcoming event more effectively in prayer? How can we get more people involved?" Then do what the Holy Spirit suggests. Remember the principle of 'more prayer is better than less,' and don't let the enemy defeat you before you have even started.

Beware of the 'let down' that follows any great event or undertaking. **Remember, God is responsible for the outcome.** We are only responsible to pray, and to walk in obedience to God. **The results are in His hands and His timing.** When great amounts of energy have been exerted, a time of vulnerability often follows. This happened to David (II Samuel 11). He let down his guard and fell into temptation with Bathsheba. Then in I Kings 18-19 we see how Elijah succumbed to the 'let down' following his great victory over the prophets of Baal.

Prayer accompanying that 'after' phase is critical. We need to be aware of the enemy's sneaky attack that comes just when we have completed our assignment. We must fill this time with new forms of prayer coverage, especially prayers of praise, worship and thanksgiving, which return the glory to God for what He has done. This prevents us from thinking the victory was anything more than our obedience to His command, and defuses our ability to take any of the credit for what has just been accomplished.

The prayer of thanksgiving 'after' allows God to pour in new strength at our weariest moments. In Isaiah he promises to give..."*Strength to the weary and increase the power of the weak...but those who hope in the LORD will renew their strength. They will soar on wings like eagles; they will run and not grow weary, they will walk and not be faint.*" *(Isa. 40:29-31)* This time of renewal in prayer 'after' is as important as the 'before' and 'during' prayer.

The Need for Prayer Activates
The Need to Pray

A quick study of Paul's life reveals two amazing truths. **First, his personal prayer life for the church illustrates his 'need to pray'.** Paul clearly expressed his heart of prayer for the local churches. *"God.....is my witness, how constantly I remember you in my prayers at all times; and I pray that now at last by God's will the way may be opened for me to come to you." (Rom. 1:9-10)* ***"Brothers, my heart's desire and prayer to God** for the Israelites is that they may be saved." (Rom. 10:1)* *"I pray that out of his glorious riches he may strengthen you with power through his Spirit in your inner being, so that Christ may dwell in your hearts through faith. And I pray that you, being rooted and established in love, may have power, together with all the saints, to grasp how wide and long and high and deep is the love of Christ..." (Eph. 3:16-18) (See also: II Tim. 1:11-12, Phil. 1:6, James 5:13-16, III John 1:2, Jude 1:20)* Paul taught the churches to pray, and modeled this by his passion to pray and intercede for the local church. He understood the vital link between the church's success and the prayer he offered. He was an intercessor who taught others the 'need to pray'.

Secondly, Paul recognized the vital link between his success and his 'need for prayer'. He actively solicited prayer *(I Thes. 5:2)* *"Finally, **brothers, pray for us** that the message of the Lord may spread.....And pray that we may be delivered from wicked and evil men, for not everyone has faith." (II Th. 3:1-2) (See also Eph. 6:19-20, Rom. 15:30-31, Eph. 6:19-20, Col. 4:3-4.)*

Many obstacles prevent the expression of the 'need for prayer'. A common misconception states that the need for prayer is somehow a sign of weakness. **In truth, asking for prayer is an expression of the character quality of humility.** Pride, which can result from a top down mentality, suggests that one must 'minister' rather than receive ministry. Independence allows for the 'no outside help is needed' attitude. In reality, we are one body where every joint supplies.

Paul continually sought prayer for his personal, health, and ministry needs, while he prayed for the needs of others. He prayed and interceded for the church, and the church in turn prayed for him.

Another dramatic Biblical illustration related to the need for prayer is recorded in Acts 12:1-17. Reading this exciting passage, we see that Peter had been thrown in prison. It appeared that soon he would be put to death for his bold proclamation of the gospel. Awaiting him was the same fate as James, who had just been martyred. Peter was in need of PRAYER! While he slept, the church mobilized. Throughout the region, word spread: Peter was in trouble. So the saints gathered in response to the 'need for prayer'.

Meanwhile, back in the prison, an angel sent to help him escape roused Peter. They quietly slipped past the guards and out of the prison. Off to the prayer meeting he went. You know the story. He knocked on the door, disturbing the prayer, but no one believed it was Peter. Finally they let him in with great rejoicing.

There is an important lesson to learn here. The local church rallied and mobilized continual prayer for as long as it took for God to answer. No doubt Peter himself prayed. But notice - at the time the answer came, he was sleeping! This story has one other interesting side note. Only the Apostle Peter and the little girl Rhoda were mentioned by name. All those supporting him in prayer were mentioned only as being part of the church that gathered together in prayer. Sounds like a closet ministry.

Jesus in the garden is another example of the 'need for prayer'. *"...Could you men not keep watch with me for one hour?" (Matt. 26:40)* This 'need for prayer' is probably the single most powerful truth related to raising up an interceding church. Please don't underestimate its power to release a church into dynamic intercession. **People pray best when a need has been identified, and**

they are moved with compassion to see that need met through their prayers.

A pastor asked me to coffee the other day, and told me all about the difficult areas he was facing. He was feeling heavily resisted, and was looking for answers. I shared with him the principle of the need for prayer. He stared at me with a glazed look in his eye, responding, "Who would want to pray for me?" So often leaders feel isolated and have difficulty asking for prayer. I reminded him of Paul's constant solicitation of prayer, and suggested he 'pull' prayer into his life. Amused, he asked what I meant by this. Without developing a great big formal program, he needed to begin to solicit prayer at every opportunity, by simply asking. This pastor had never considered, in all his years of ministry, the concept of 'pulling in' prayer.

The need for prayer is great, but there is a certain vulnerability that goes along with the asking. Humility defuses pride. It allows others to enter into your battles and God's hand to move on your behalf. This humility lets others be engaged in prayer who would not be otherwise. It is one of the greatest steps you can take toward raising up an interceding church.

There is a trust that comes when we are open to receiving prayer from others. Think about it. If everyone who needs prayer is afraid to ask, then the end result is no one praying. Without information, no intelligent intercession can take place. Without fuel to feed the fires of prayer, they soon go out.

If every Christian asked just two people to intercede for them, immediately the church would be activated to a new level of prayer. There is a multiplication effect that takes place. The enemy does not want to see this happen; he knows that there is a real power in agreement. The Bible says, *"... if two of you on earth agree about anything you ask for, it will be done for you by my Father in heaven."* (Matt. 18:19)

Our own flesh and fallen nature do not like to be humble or express a need, which might be perceived as weakness. Paul said, *"For when I am weak, then I am strong."* (II Cor. 12:10) This weakness can lead to strength when we reach out to others and stand in agreement. Next time you run into a difficulty, pull prayer into your life. Call on your family, friends or pastors to stand with you in prayer. Fight pride, and give God a chance to intervene, while increasing someone else's prayer life. Remember, the more prayers, the more the answers.

No matter the size of the Church, this simple tool can be used to raise the level of prayer. The need for prayer and the request made for it enables even greater numbers of the Body of Christ to be involved in fulfilling the purposes of God. The success of today's leaders, like the leaders of old, is dependent upon the prayer coverage they receive from the saints.

Prayer is also a valuable unifying factor in the church. It is difficult to pray and then complain about someone or something at the same time. People that pray together, stay together. Prayer brings resistance to division, disloyalty and disunity. It draws the body together, creating interdependence upon one another. We should follow Paul's example and develop, at all levels, a 'need for prayer', which activates in others the 'need to pray'.

These principles are meant to be an encouragement to you in your personal prayer life as well as in your local church. Spend some time pondering each one and ask the Lord to speak to you. Write down the ideas He gives you in each area. Begin to knead these principles into your life and the life of the church. Continue to fan, lead and direct prayer and intercession. Dedicate special services to Prayer and Praise. Call times of All Church Fasts. Encourage prayer at every level.

Develop these powerful seed truths, and plant them carefully in good soil. You will begin to see the fruit as you water and fertilize these principles. Do not let their simplicity undermine their incredible potential to raise up an interceding church. Remember, every tree comes from just one tiny seed. Then it goes on to produce millions more seeds, each one capable of producing another mighty tree. What an awesome concept! Prepare the soil, plant the seeds of God's Word, and watch them grow. Be careful to protect, guard and nurture what is growing until a great harvest in prayer is realized.

Scripture shows us that every believer can be an intercessor, and every church is to be an interceding church. The garden illustration relates directly to this entire process. We must move beyond individual prayers or isolated prayer groups, bringing the total church in response to the call to pray. **The church is the instrument of God to fulfill His purpose in the earth today.**

Resistance against prayer makes it abundantly clear that prayer ministry in the church will not grow without direct, intentional oversight and leadership. God has planted prayer in the garden of our local church, and we are responsible to cultivate and protect it until it reaches fruitfulness.

Take time now and in the coming days to review your notes. It is my prayer that God will continue to minister to you as you grow in your own prayer journey. May God richly bless you. Let the Holy Spirit be your guide in raising up an interceding church, one person at a time. May God richly bless you.

Steps for Releasing
Prayer in the Local Church

There will be no interceding churches without interceding leadership. Isolated groups can never initiate and sustain enough prayer thrust. These people can be great inspirations, and provide prayer leadership, but they cannot create and maintain the overall momentum. Prayer must be more than just a doctrinal statement recorded and filed somewhere.

Without the senior leadership moving prayer forward in a systematic manner, it will soon lose momentum and die out. Since a congregation reflects the leadership, it will be evident if the leaders are truly passionate about prayer, or merely giving lip service. Passion fuels prayer, and leadership provides the structure to sustain its growth.

Lay the foundation - the Word of God. Teach and preach extensively on prayer and intercession, raising awareness and laying a solid foundation in the Body.

Create a "Place to Pray", facilitating prayer for individuals and groups, seven days a week. Dedicate a Prayer Center to increase the level of exposure and provide a space for prayer.

Raise the profile of prayer in the congregation. Deliberately bring prayer and intercession into every service. Opening Service Intercession differs from pre-service prayer in that it begins the service, taking place in the main auditorium, so the whole congregation participates. Dedicating the first 15-20 minutes of the service to prayer fulfills Matt. 21:13: *"...My House shall be called a house of prayer."*

Install Prayer Pastors and a prayer leadership team to provide leadership and oversight to the prayer and intercessory activities. Continue to call upon the congregation to pray, fast, and grow as intercessors.

Encourage regional and city prayer, as the Lord shows you opportunities. Breakfast meetings and monthly city Pastors' prayer meetings are ways to increase unity, relationship and prayer.

Prayer Leadership Qualifications

Whether the church is small or large, a prayer pastor is essential. The selection must agree with the spiritual and character qualifications set out in scripture for leadership, as stated in I Timothy. Much depends upon the ability of this leader to motivate and inspire people to greater levels of prayer. His or her primary focus must be that of devotion to the local church and its vision. Spiritual maturity means consistently giving the glory to God for the results of answered prayer. This person or couple may serve as lay leaders or be on full-time staff, but their commitment to the local church must be central.

Prayer Pastor: Sample Job Description

1. Meet monthly with your Senior Pastor to know his heart, his prayer concerns.
2. Meet monthly with the Prayer Leadership Team to pray, encourage, motivate, and communicate.
3. Be faithful with your assignments.
4. Realize that follow-through is important.
5. Systematically encourage prayer throughout the church.
6. Work to bring all team members to their fullest potential in prayer. Target every age group for growth in prayer, being careful that no group is suppressed or excluded.
7. Develop an annual church calendar for prayer events, training opportunities, special meetings, etc. Distribute it to the whole church.
8. Only start what you have leadership to cover - through all five stages of vision, strategy, implementation, results and maintenance.
9. Be positive, persistent and tenacious. Remember: Prayer is the MOST resisted activity on the planet.
10. Be an encourager. Show people how God wants to answer their prayers.

Prayer Ministry Team: Basic Qualifications

1. Above all, have a vision for the local church.
2. Be submitted to the leadership of that church.
3. Be able to put the vision of the church above personal agendas.
4. Have a strong love for the people.
5. Possess a servant's heart.
6. Be adjustable.
7. Have a humble spirit and attitude.
8. Be able to teach, motivate and inspire others.
9. Have organizational skills.
10. Be able to delegate and get others involved.

Prayer Ministry requires a balanced team of men and women, singles, and married couples, including various age groups. No one person can fulfill the role of prayer Pastor in a local church. Because of the great responsibility, it takes a team!

These tape series on prayer by Frank Damazio are also available through City Bible Publishing.
(Phone 1-800-777-6057)
• The Seven Power Points of Prayer
• Gap Standing and Hedge Building

Footnotes

1 Conner, Kevin. The Tabernacle of Moses, Bible Press, Portland OR, page 47
2 Conner, Kevin. The Tabernacle of Moses. Bible Press. Portland, OR page 53
3 Damazio, Frank. Gap Standing and Hedge Building. City Bible Publishing. Portland, OR